AGuide for Using

Stone Fox

in the Classroom

**Based on the novel written by
John Reynolds Gardiner**

D1551215

This guide written by **Pat Angell, Peg Isakson,
Jeannine Myers, Donna Shay**

Teacher Created Materials, Inc.
6421 Industry Way
Westminster, CA 92683
www.teachercreated.com
©*1996 Teacher Created Materials, Inc.*
Reprinted, 2002
Made in U.S.A.
ISBN-1-55734-567-8

Edited by
Judith Brewer

Illustrated by
Jose L. Tapia

Cover Art by
Norm Merritt

Table of Contents

Introduction

A good book can touch our lives like a good friend. Within its pages are words and characters that can inspire us to achieve our highest ideals. We can turn to it for companionship, recreation, comfort, and guidance. It can also give us a cherished story to hold in our hearts forever.

In *Literature Units*, great care has been taken to select books that are sure to become good friends.

Teachers who use this literature unit will find the following features to supplement their own valuable ideas.

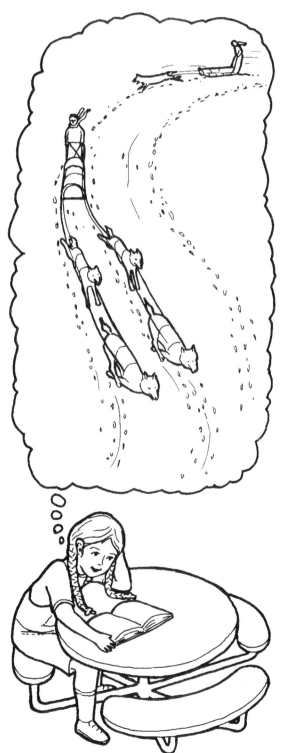

- A Sample Lesson Plan

- Pre-reading Activities

- A Biographical Sketch and Picture of the Author

- A Book Summary

- Vocabulary Lists

- Vocabulary Activity Ideas

- Lessons grouped for study with each section including:

  - *quizzes*

  - *hands-on projects*

  - *cooperative learning activities*

  - *cross-curriculum connections*

  - *extensions into the reader's life*

- Post-reading Activities

- Book Report Ideas

- Culminating Activities

- Three Different Options for Unit Tests

- A Bibliography

- An Answer Key

We are confident that this unit will be a valuable addition to your planning, and we hope that as you use our ideas, your students will increase the circle of "friends" they have in books!

Sample Lesson Plan

Each of the lessons below can take from one to several days to complete.

LESSON 1

- Introduce and complete some or all of the pre-reading activities. (page 5)
- Read "About the Author" with your students. (page 6)
- Introduce the vocabulary list for Section 1. (page 8)

LESSON 2

- Read chapters 1 and 2. As you read, place the vocabulary words in the context of the story and discuss their meanings.
- Choose a vocabulary activity. (page 9)
- Organize discussion groups with the questions for Section 1. (page 10)
- Make twice-baked potatoes. (page 13)
- Research Wyoming with a map. (page 14)
- Create Willy Webs. (page 15)
- Illustrate Grandfather's Portrait. (page 16)
- Administer the Section 1 quiz. (page 12)
- Introduce the vocabulary list for Section 2. (page 8)

LESSON 3

- Read chapters 3 and 4. Place vocabulary words in context and discuss their meanings.
- Choose a vocabulary activity. (page 9)
- Make Discussion Cubes. (page 18)
- Organize discussion groups with the questions for Section 2 (page 10) or the questions on the discussion cubes.
- Create a story mobile or group collage. (page 19)
- Create racing team practice charts and bar graphs. (page 20)
- Write a daily schedule for little Willy. (page 21)
- Administer the Section 2 quiz. (page 17)
- Introduce the vocabulary list for Section 3. (page 8)

LESSON 4

- Read chapters 5 and 6. Place vocabulary words in context and discuss their meanings.
- Choose a vocabulary activity. (page 9)
- Organize discussion groups with the questions for Section 3. (pages 10 and 11)
- Create T-shirts and hats for the race. (page 23)
- Use a Venn diagram to compare characters. (page 24)

- Learn about growing potatoes. (page 25)
- Study taxes. (page 26)
- Administer the Section 3 quiz. (page 22)
- Introduce the vocabulary list for Section 4. (page 8)

LESSON 5

- Read chapters 7 and 8. Place vocabulary words in context and discuss their meanings.
- Choose a vocabulary activity. (page 9)
- Organize discussion groups with the questions for Section 4. (page 11)
- Create hand or stick puppets of the characters. (page 28)
- Complete the Wyoming Animal Report. (page 29)
- Learn about genre. (pages 30)
- Explore your Spuds à la Carte. (page 31)
- Administer the Section 4 quiz. (page 27)
- Introduce the vocabulary list for Section 5. (page 8)

LESSON 6

- Read chapters 9 and 10. Place vocabulary words in context and discuss their meanings.
- Choose a vocabulary activity. (page 9)
- Organize discussion groups with the questions for Section 5. (page 11)
- Create a landmarks mural of the race course. (page 33)
- Discuss thoughts and create Thinking Clouds. (page 34)
- Write about Searchlight's qualities. (page 35)
- Create lists for characters and you. (page 36)
- Administer the Section 5 quiz. (page 32)

LESSON 7

- Discuss any questions your students may have about the story. (page 37)
- Assign book reports. (page 38)
- Begin work on culminating activities. (pages 39–42)

LESSON 8

- Administer unit tests, 1, 2, and/or 3. (pages 43, 44, 45)
- Discuss the test answers and possibilities.
- Discuss the students' enjoyment of the book.
- Provide a list of related reading for your students. (page 46)

Before the Book

Your students will be eager to read *Stone Fox* after they spend some time discussing what they know about having dogs as pets, dogsled races, and attempts by children to earn extra money. Basic pre-reading strategies will activate their prior knowledge and set the scene for the story to follow. A personal connection with parts of a story will enhance students' comprehension and enjoyment of literature.

The following pre-reading activities may work well with your class.

1. Discuss with students any experiences they may have had with dogs as pets in their families. Ask if there was anything special in the dog/child relationship that was heartwarming.

2. Conduct a brainstorming session on dogsled races. Ask students to suggest any words that come to mind when you present the words "dogsled race." Accept any words that are offered and cluster them on the chalkboard as they are given. Keep these words on chart paper for later use.

3. Investigate the possibility of dogsled races in your state or in other states where they would possibly be held.

4. Have students share what they know about growing potatoes as a farm crop. Ask the following questions:

   — *What states might grow potatoes as a crop?*
   — *What kind of growing conditions would be necessary?*

5. Use a map to show the state of Wyoming, where *Stone Fox* takes place. Discuss the feasibility of potato farming and dogsled racing in the state.

6. Define a legend. Ask students if they have heard any legends about dogs in their families or found any in other readings.

7. Discuss the title *Stone Fox.* Make predictions about the use of the words. Ask for interpretations of the title.

8. Preview the book by reading the front and back covers, the title page, and the dedication. Make predictions about the content.

9. Preview all the illustrations throughout the story. Generate group questions for each illustration.

About the Author

John Reynolds Gardiner was born on December 6, 1944, in Los Angeles, California. His parents were both educators and wanted very much for him to be a good student. At the time, though, he rebelled and refused to read. The more his mother insisted he read, the more he refused. She did read aloud to him, though, sometimes against his wishes. He would pretend to be asleep, but as soon as he became engrossed in the story, he wouldn't want her to stop. He didn't read his first novel by himself until he was nineteen years old!

Even though he was a nonreader as a child and proclaimed himself very poor at spelling and grammar, his stories showed he had a lively imagination and humor. Sometimes his teachers didn't believe he had written them by himself. When he was in high school, one of his teachers told him he would not make it through college English, but he proved that teacher wrong.

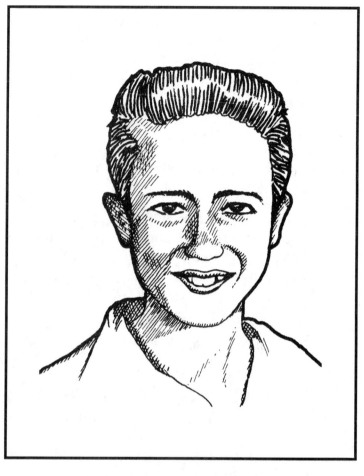

John Reynolds Gardiner at the age of 11.

Mr. Gardiner graduated from the University of California in Los Angeles with a Masters Degree in Engineering. He has traveled widely, living and working in Europe, Central America, and Idaho, where he first heard the legend that is the basis for *Stone Fox*. He now works as an engineer in California, predicting the temperature of satellites, and does his writing on his lunch break. He gives seminars on writing and marketing children's books at colleges and universities and has adapted stories for children's television programs. He is also an inventor for Num Num Novelty Company. Mr. Gardiner and his wife have three daughters and live in Huntington Beach, California.

Stone Fox is his first published work. It has won several awards, has been translated into three foreign languages, and has been made into a 1987 NBC television movie. Other books he has written are *Top Secret, General Butterfingers,* and *The Last Secret.*

Mr. Gardiner thinks it is very important to encourage beginning writers, even if they are not good at spelling and grammar, and he says, "Thank you, Mom, for not giving up on me, for your rebel son is now a reader, a writer, and a lover of books."

(Sources used: *Fourth Book of Junior Authors* and *Something About the Author:* Volume 64)

6

Stone Fox

by John Reynolds Gardiner
(Crowell, 1980)

(Canada and UK, Harper Collins Publishers Ltd.; AUS, Harper Collins)

Little Willy lived with his grandfather on a small potato farm in Wyoming. One morning Grandfather would not get out of bed. Usually Grandfather was the first one up and had breakfast made before little Willy stirred, so Willy was worried. He took his dog, Searchlight, and went down the road to get Doc Smith. She examined Grandfather but could find nothing wrong with him. "I'm sorry child," she said, "but it appears that your grandfather just doesn't want to live anymore."

Little Willy was determined to make Grandfather want to live again. The potato crop was ready for harvest, and Willy managed to do it alone by hitching Searchlight to the plow. But the tax man was a bigger problem. He said the taxes hadn't been paid for ten years, and they owed about five hundred dollars. Either Grandfather had to pay the taxes or the farm would be sold. Willy decided to save the farm—the only question was "how?" Then he heard about the National Dogsled Races with a cash prize of five hundred dollars. He used his college savings account for the entrance fee, and he and Searchlight began practicing for the race.

Stone Fox, the legendary winner of past races, arrived in town and also entered the race. The Native American had five beautiful Samoyeds, a fearsome reputation, and was every bit as intent on winning the prize money as little Willy.

There was a great deal of excitement on the day of the race. Would little Willy win the race and save the farm and his grandfather? Would Stone Fox or one of the other entrants win? An unexpected turn of events during the race stunned the whole town and created a moving conclusion to the story.

Vocabulary Lists

The vocabulary words listed below correspond to each section of *Stone Fox*, as outlined in the table of contents. Ideas for vocabulary activities are found on page 9 of this book.

Section 1
(Chapters 1–2)

explanation	credit	irrigation
harmonica	situation	directly
palomino	harness	plow
proceeded	acre	strongbox
examination	surrounded	mature
code	harvest	determined
mended	concerned	bushel

Section 2
(Chapters 3–4)

crisp	official	ricocheting
gully	taxes	authority
exhausted	sturdy	legal
derringer	enabled	lunged

Section 3
(Chapters 5–6)

varied	homeland	constructed
Samoyed	reservation	tilted
entrance fee	bobbled	awesome
amateurs	represented	tribe
moccasins	stunned	contestants
legends	lightly	clutching

Section 4
(Chapters 7–8)

embarrassed	clenched	jagged
deserted	rooting	city slickers
swollen	treacherous	tension
abrupt halt	massive	abreast

Section 5
(Chapters 9–10)

attempted	challenger	regained
glimpse	inching	suffering
forged	disqualified	effortlessly

8

Vocabulary Activity Ideas

The vocabulary suggested by students in the pre-reading activities and the vocabulary selected from *Stone Fox* (page 8 of this book) will form a student-teacher list of vocabulary words to enhance comprehension of the story. Interesting vocabulary activities will help students integrate those words into their everyday language. The ideas below will help your students learn and use those words.

❏ Have students choose one word that is new to them from the *Stone Fox* vocabulary list. The word chosen should be a noun: a person, place, or thing. The student creates a **Concept Definition Word Map** (or CD Map) by following the procedure below to create a graphic organizer.

Write the new word in a circle centered on a page. Working outward, use spokes to connect the new-word circle to other circles or boxes with these labels on them: Category (What is it?), Properties (What is it like?), Comparisons (What is similar to this word?), Descriptions (What are some examples?), and Opposites (What is opposite to the new word?). Next, fill in the boxes with answers to the questions.

❏ Have students choose one of the new words from the vocabulary lists presented. Create a **Concept Circle** by making a circle on a blank page with a protractor or by tracing around a round object. Divide the circle into four pie-shaped sections. Put the new word on a line drawn at the top of the circle. Think of three other words that mean almost the same as your top word. Put them in the sections of your circle. Think of one word that is not the same, but might be very close to the meaning. Put it in the fourth section. Ask your classmates to identify the word that does not go with the others! Here is an example: new word = inspected, four words in circle = examined, scrutinized, perused, glanced. The word that does not go with the others is "glanced." This activity invites dictionary or thesaurus work and stimulates vocabulary conversations among students.

❏ Have each student choose three words from the vocabulary lists and create a **Word Sort**. For each word chosen, think of four additional words that would fit in the same category. Example: the key word is palomino, and the four other words are bay, paint, sorrel, black (all colors of horses). Mix up the 12 additional words. Ask a friend to sort the 12 words under the three key words.

❏ Have students create **Alphables** by listing the words in alphabetical order and dividing them into syllables.

❏ Copy selected sentences or paragraphs from *Stone Fox*, leaving out important vocabulary words and creating a **Concept Cloze** activity. Have a group brainstorming session to suggest a variety of words to fill in the blanks, using context clues. Present the author's choice of word.

❏ Keep a **Word Wall** in your room. When students find a new vocabulary word in their reading, have them write the new word, its definition, and a sentence using the word on an index card or sentence strip. Staple it to a bulletin board set aside for this purpose.

❏ Ask your students to create an **Illustrated Dictionary** of the vocabulary words. This could be an individual or group activity. Have students write the vocabulary words and draw a simple picture showing what each word means.

Discussion Guide

The following questions are not meant to be part of a "read and answer the question" style of teaching. Rather, they should be used for group discussions and sharing of responses in literature circles that explore the story. Dialogue is an effective method for teaching and learning about literature by guiding the process of interpreting or understanding what we read. In contrast, writing out answers to questions becomes more of a check on accuracy and a product of comprehension.

A synopsis of each section and group discussion starters follow.

Chapters 1 and 2

Synopsis:

The setting is a potato farm in Wyoming. Little Willy, Grandfather, and Willy's dog, Searchlight, work hard on this farm. Willy, in his free time, races Searchlight around the town with a dogsled. Grandfather becomes ill.

Discussion:

- What do you think it would be like to live with a grandparent?
- Think about what it would be like to live on a potato farm. What might some of your responsibilities or chores be?
- What words describe Willy? Grandfather? Searchlight?
- How do you think Willy and Grandfather work together as a family? Why?

Chapters 3 and 4

Synopsis:

A tax collector arrives and tells Willy that Grandfather owes 10 years worth of back taxes amounting to $500. Either Grandfather pays the taxes or the farm will be sold.

Discussion:

- What responsibilities on the farm will Willy take over? What responsibilities do you have with your family?
- What do you think it would be like not to have enough money to pay your bills?
- What do you think it would be like to lose your home because your parents couldn't pay their taxes?
- Think about what Willy must feel when he discovers Grandfather didn't pay the taxes.

Chapters 5 and 6

Synopsis:

Willy is determined to save the farm but doesn't have enough money. Then Willy hears about the National Dogsled Race and decides to enter the race, hoping to win the prize money. To enter the race, Willy uses his education money for the fee. Searchlight and Willy practice racing. Stone Fox, the legendary winner of past races, arrives in town and enters the race. The Indian drives five beautiful Samoyeds and holds a fearsome reputation.

Discussion Guide *(cont.)*

═══════ **Chapters 5 and 6** *(cont.)* ═══════

Discussion:

- Lots of people gave Willy advice. What advice is given? Do you think it is good advice?
- How do you think the townspeople feel about Willy?
- What makes Willy feel "ten feet tall" when he steps out of the City Hall building?
- What would your feelings be if you met a legendary competitor?

═══════ **Chapters 7 and 8** ═══════

Synopsis:

While Willy is returning home from running an errand the night before the race, he hears dogs barking in an old barn. Willy discovers Stone Fox's Samoyeds. Stone Fox sees Willy with his dogs and hits him in the face. Neither Willy nor Searchlight sleep that night.

The day of the race arrives and although Willy's eye is swollen shut, he still feels like a winner. Willy gives Stone Fox a friendly greeting despite the night before. Excitement builds in anticipation of the race. The race begins.

Discussion:

- What words would you use to describe Stone Fox?
- Why do you think Stone Fox hit Willy?
- Even though Willy is injured, he still is sure he will win the race.
- How do you think Grandfather is feeling on the day of the race?

═══════ **Chapters 9 and 10** ═══════

Synopsis:

Willy surges ahead while Stone Fox remains last. At the home stretch, however, Stone Fox matches Willy's speed, and the two racers rush toward the finish line. Searchlight forges ahead, but just short of the finish line, she dies. Stone Fox stops racing, checks Searchlight, and then, after considering his next move, he draws a line in the snow, pulls out his rifle, and threatens to shoot anyone who crosses the finish line. He looks at Willy, who then carries Searchlight over the finish line to win the race.

Discussion:

- What things happen in the race that make Willy gain and then lose speed?
- When tragedy happens, people express their feelings in different ways. How are you feeling about Searchlight's death?
- What might Grandfather and Willy talk about after the race?
- Name some clues that tell you Stone Fox has some very deep feelings even though his speech and facial expressions do not show them.

Quiz Time

1. On the back of this paper, write a one-paragraph summary of the major events in chapters one and two. Then complete the rest of the questions on this page.

2. Grandfather loves to play tricks on little Willy. What is the trick that makes Grandfather laugh until he cries?

   _____

   _____

3. Why does little Willy find his plate in the chicken coop one morning?

   _____

   _____

4. What does little Willy say to Doc Smith that causes her to believe that something is seriously wrong with Grandfather?

   _____

   _____

5. Why do you think Grandfather's beard is full of tears as he lies in bed?

   _____

   _____

6. What does Doc Smith believe is wrong with Grandfather?

   _____

   _____

7. Little Willy and Grandfather work out a way to communicate with each other without Grandfather talking. How do they do that?

   _____

   _____

8. How do little Willy and Searchlight manage to harvest the crop of potatoes?

   _____

   _____

   _____

9. Tell about Searchlight's intelligence in one well-written sentence.

   _____

   _____

10. On the back of this paper, tell about your predictions regarding Grandfather's illness, Doc Smith's recommendations, and little Willy's determination to keep the family together.

Something's Cooking

Little Willy and Grandfather live on a potato farm. Each year when they have a good potato crop, they sell potatoes to the people in the community. There are many ways to fix potatoes. A popular recipe is Twice-baked Potatoes. The following is a version of this recipe.

Twice-baked Potatoes

Ingredients:

- potatoes (For each potato cooked you will need the following amounts of cheese, onions, and sour cream.)
  - $\frac{1}{2}$ slice of cheese
  - $\frac{1}{8}$ cup (31 mL) chopped or minced onions
  - $\frac{1}{4}$ cup (63 mL) sour cream

Equipment:

- aluminum foil
- oven (or coals, if using a campfire)
- knife
- bowl
- wooden spoon
- measuring cup

Directions:

1. Scrub potatoes until skins are clean and wrap each potato in a piece of aluminum foil.
2. Put the wrapped potato in campfire coals or in a kitchen oven for approximately one hour at 350° Fahrenheit (180° Celsius).
3. Remove the potatoes from the heat. Let them cool for 15 minutes.
4. Cut the potatoes lengthwise and scoop out the pulp or softened potato, into a bowl. Save the skins.
5. Add the appropriate amounts of sour cream and onions (see above) to the potatoes and mix the ingredients.
6. Put some of the mixture into each of the potato skins.
7. Top each potato with half a slice of cheese and heat the potatoes for 15 minutes to melt the cheese.

Extension:

Find other potato recipes and make a potato cookbook. Make your cookbook in the shape of a potato. Think about how Grandfather and little Willy might have fixed potatoes to eat. Discuss whether or not each recipe you have found could be one that little Willy and Grandfather would fix. Why or why not?

Roaming Wyoming

Stone Fox takes place in the small town of Jackson in the state of Wyoming. The word "Wyoming" came from changes made to a Delaware Indian word for "upon the great plain." It helps you understand the characters and their actions in a story if you know more than the book tells you about where the story takes place.

Activity 1—Getting to Know Wyoming

- In a classroom discussion group, think of all the things you already know about Wyoming. Make a chart and list the things you believe are true about Wyoming.
- Next, think of the things you would like to know about Wyoming and make a list of the questions.
- List the resources you could use to find answers to your questions.

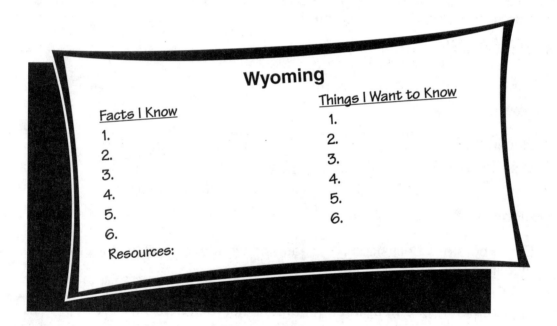

Activity 2—Map Skills

- Research to find the shape of Wyoming, its bordering states, and the mountain ranges located in and around Wyoming.

- Complete the following tasks and report your findings to the class.

  1. Use a map to find Jackson, Wyoming, where the story of *Stone Fox* takes place. Locate the Wind River Reservation where the Shoshone and Arapaho North American Indian tribes lived together after the Shoshone were forced to leave Utah. Stone Fox belonged to the Shoshone tribe and might have lived there.

  2. Plan the route across Wyoming that you think Stone Fox might have taken to get from the reservation to Jackson for the National Dogsled Race. Write your directions as if you were telling Stone Fox what route to take. Use mountain ranges, rivers, compass directions (N, S, E, W) and estimated mileage in your directions.

Willy Web

Think of words that describe Willy and his actions in the story section(s) that you have read. On this page, the first two boxes are filled in with "persistent" and "hardworking." They are words that tell something about Willy. Look in the story to find the phrases or sentences that the author uses to show, or tell more about, how Willy was persistent or hardworking. Put those page numbers or phrases on the lines under "persistent" and "hardworking." Now think of four more descriptive words to fill in the boxes and then find the pages and phrases where the author told more to help you understand the description.

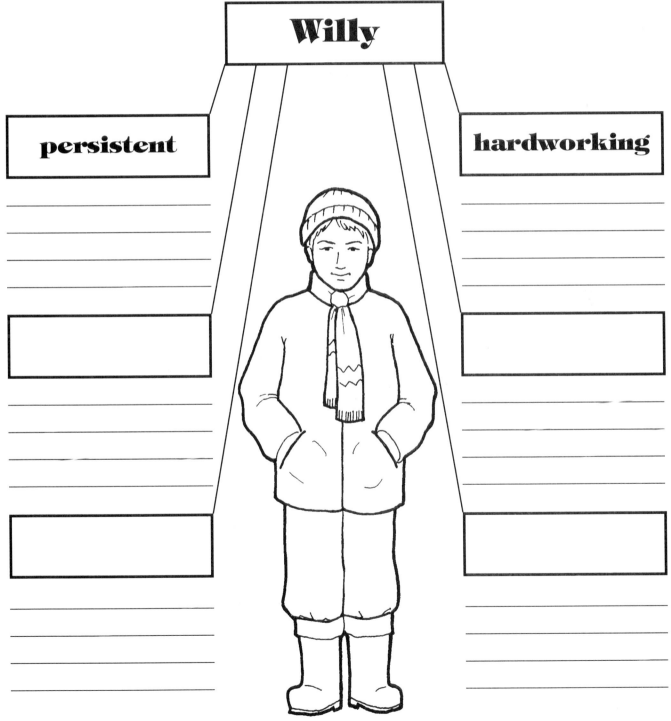

Grandfather's Portrait

Find clues and hints in the story as to what Grandfather looked like before he got sick. In the frame on the right, illustrate Grandfather as a younger man.

Biographical Sketch:

Write two or three paragraphs about Grandfather when he was healthy. Once again, there are many clues in the story about what Grandfather was like, even when he was younger. Use your knowledge of the times in which he lived and your imagination to describe Grandfather. Remember, Grandfather was a different kind of person before the tax problem came up.

Think of a grandparent or an older friend or neighbor you know. In the frame on the left, illustrate that person.

Biographical Sketch:

Write two or three paragraphs about this person as you know him or her. Include some ideas about how Grandfather and your person are alike and/or how they are different.

Quiz Time

1. On the back of this paper, write a one-paragraph summary of the major events in chapters 3 and 4. Then complete the rest of the questions on this page.

2. What is Grandfather's advice about asking questions?

   _____

   _____

   _____

3. How does little Willy get ready for winter?

   _____

   _____

4. Why has Grandfather put some money away in a savings account?

   _____

   _____

5. After school little Willy and Searchlight go into the town of Jackson to run errands. Tell about the "race" they run each day at 6:00.

   _____

   _____

6. Who is waiting for little Willy when he arrives home?

   _____

   _____

7. How does Grandfather respond to the visitors?

   _____

   _____

   _____

8. Characterize Clifford Snyder in one well-written sentence.

   _____

   _____

   _____

9. What is the message that Clifford Snyder leaves with Grandfather and little Willy?

   _____

   _____

10. On the back of this paper, write about your feelings regarding the predicament that little Willy is in now.

Discussion Cubes

Think of six questions about the story that you have read so far. Remember to ask different kinds of questions; for example, a "think and search" question can be answered by thinking about different parts of the story and putting information together.

Make a discussion cube from the pattern below. Cut out the cube on the solid lines only. Write one question on each side of the box. Carefully fold the dashed lines. With cellophane tape, secure the tabs in the cube so it will resemble a closed box.

In a literature discussion group, take turns gently rolling the cubes and responding to the questions that appear on top.

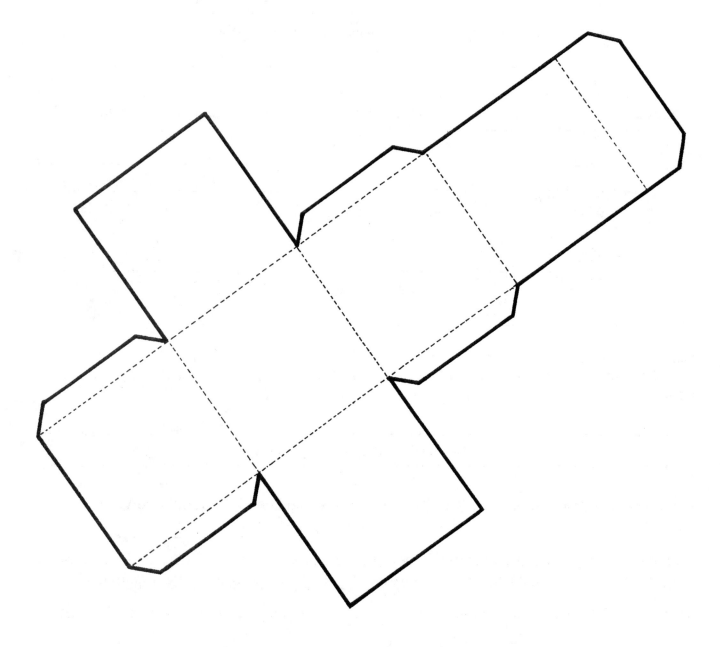

Creative Starts with Art

Create a Story Mobile

In a cooperative learning group, begin collecting artifacts, illustrations, or printed material that have a connection with *Stone Fox*. Share your collections in your group and decide if you have artifacts that would create one of the following:

- individual thematic mobiles (i.e., potato farming or Wyoming or story elements)
- one large mobile that would depict all of the story by the end of the unit

Use a clothes hanger for the thematic mobile or several clothes hangers wired together for a complete story mobile. Arrange and secure the artifacts with string or wire so they hang in balance.

Create a Group Collage

In your cooperative learning group, collect, arrange, and glue a collection of magazine or newspaper clippings and pictures that would have a connection with *Stone Fox.*

Begin the arrangement in one corner of a large piece of paper. As you continue to read the story, collect additional pieces and add to your collage in sequence around the paper.

Your group will need to come to an agreement for the sequence and arrangement of pieces.

On Your Mark . . . Get Set . . .

To prepare for an upcoming dogsled race, several teams practice routinely. On the average, each dogsled team practices five miles per day. Suppose each team practiced three days. Their times for each practice run are recorded on the chart below.

Interpret the Data

Use the information in this chart to answer the questions below.

Day	Sled 1	Sled 2	Sled 3	Sled 4
1	35 min.	40 min.	39 min.	34 min.
2	30 min.	44 min.	37 min.	39 min.
3	38 min.	31 min.	30 min.	30 min.

1. What is each team's average time?_____

2. Who has the highest average? _____

3. What was the lowest average? _____

4. How many dogsled teams average the same time? _____

5. If the real race is 45 miles long, on the average how long will it take the teams to finish the race? _____

Extension:

1. The median is halfway between two points. What is the median time for the sleds on each day?

   Day 1_____ Day 2_____ Day 3_____

2. The mode is the value occurring most frequently in a set of data. What is the mode for all of the sleds, including all of the days?_____

Create a Bar Graph

In the story *Stone Fox*, five beautiful Samoyeds form the sled team for the legendary Indian, Stone Fox. People like different breeds of dogs for different reasons. Follow these guidelines to create your own graph of people's favorites.

• Make a list of several favorite breeds of dogs.

• Survey your classmates to see which breed of dog is the most popular.

• Display your findings in a bar graph. Then express the results in fraction sentences. **(Example:** Three-fourths of the people I asked said that a Samoyed is their favorite breed.)

Willy's Schedule

Most children and adults have certain things they need to do almost every day. Think about your daily schedule. Think of a typical school day and the things you usually do.

Now choose a school day from *Stone Fox,* a day after Grandfather got sick. On the lines below, taking clues from Willy's experiences in the book, list the times of day and the activities that you think make up Willy's usual schedule for a full day.

Example: **Willy's Day**

Time	Activity
6:30 A.M.	Get out of bed and make a fire.
6:45 A.M.	Fix oatmeal mush.

When you have finished, share your schedule for Willy in a literature discussion group. Share your insights and understandings about the schedule and the responsibilities you discover that Willy probably has.

Time	Activity

Quiz Time

1. On the back of this paper, write a one-paragraph summary of the major events in chapters 5 and 6. Then complete the questions on the rest of the page.

2. What is meant by the statement "Where there's a will, there's a way"?

   _____

   _____

   _____

3. Mr. Foster at the bank advises Willy to sell the farm. Why do you think he gives that advice?

   _____

   _____

4. Tell about the idea Willy gets to make some money after he visits Lester's General Store.

   _____

   _____

5. Do you believe that Grandfather would agree with what Willy is trying to do?

   _____

   _____

6. How does Willy pay for his entrance fee for the race?

   _____

   _____

7. Willy feels strong and good until he sees something at the end of the street. Describe what he sees.

   _____

   _____

8. Why doesn't Stone Fox speak to anyone?

   _____

   _____

9. What is Stone Fox's dream for his people?

   _____

   _____

   _____

10. On the back of this paper, explain what you would do now if you were little Willy.

Let's Enter the Race

Imagine that the dogsled races are coming to your town! Everyone who enters will receive a T-shirt and a hat for participating in this great race. Design a dogsled race T-shirt, using the pattern below. Create a hat out of construction paper for each person who pays the entrance fee.

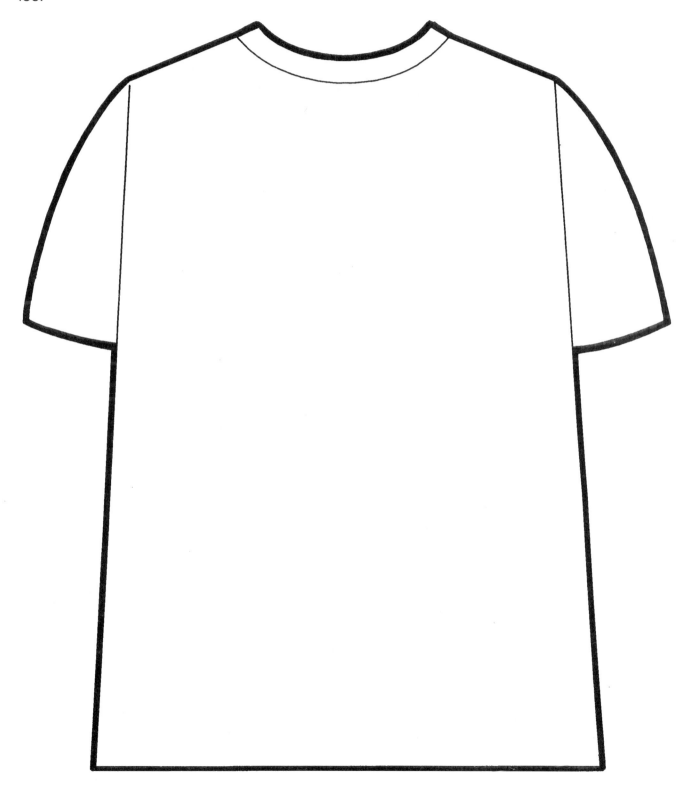

Character Comparison

In the story, *Stone Fox*, little Willy and Stone Fox seem to have some common attributes. In a cooperative learning group, brainstorm some ways that the two characters are alike and some ways that they are different. Record your findings on the Venn diagram below.

In the intersecting center of the circles, write the things both characters have in common. In the outer parts of the circles, write some things that make them different.

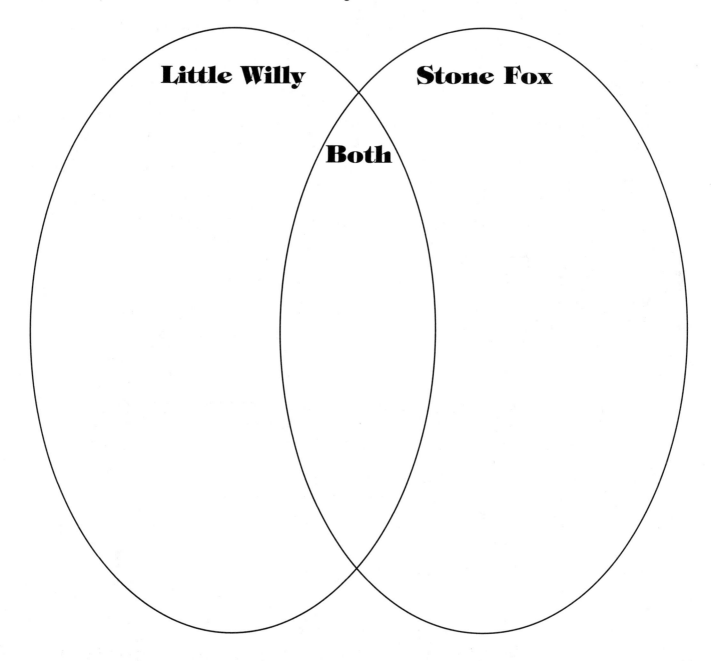

Extension:

Create a Venn diagram comparing yourself to little Willy, or compare little Willy to someone you know.

Growing Potatoes

"But the potatoes barely bring in enough money to live on," explained little Willy. "We went broke last year."

Little Willy is concerned that growing potatoes will not provide enough income for Grandfather to pay his taxes and get out of debt. How hard is it to grow potatoes and have a successful crop?

Think about what you already know or would predict about growing potatoes. Put an X in front of your choices below.

1. Potatoes grow

   (a) on bushes.
   (b) underground.
   (c) on trees.

2. Potatoes need

   (a) flat ground to grow on.
   (b) little holes or depressions to grow in.
   (c) a mound of dirt around each plant.

3. New potato plants come from

   (a) little seeds in packages.
   (b) a special piece of another potato.
   (c) a leaf cutting from a grown plant.

4. Potatoes are grown

   (a) only in the United States and Canada.
   (b) only in South America.
   (c) in almost all the countries of the world.

5. A piece of potato tastes

   (a) sweet.
   (b) bitter.
   (c) bland. (very little flavor)

6. How many kinds of potatoes would you predict there are?

   (a) two   (c) fourteen
   (b) five   (d) thirty

There are many resources for finding out about potatoes. Some places are libraries, state potato grower organizations, and interviews with farmers or gardeners. Use your resources to find the answers to your predictions above and to learn the growing stages of a potato.

In the boxes below, draw the five stages of a potato plant.

planting	the new plant begins	the young plant	rhizomes & tubers	ready for harvest

Now go back to your predictions about growing potatoes. Would you change any of your answers now that you have used your resources? If so, use a colored pen to circle your new answers.

Taxing Questions

Grandfather is about to lose his farm because for each of the past ten years, he has not paid his taxes. To understand this story better, we need to know more about taxes.

What are taxes? A tax is a charge on a person's income or property made by the government to collect revenue, or dollars. The revenue is used by the government to provide services to the population and to the communities. Grandfather was required by the state of Wyoming to pay taxes on his property each year.

Activities:

1. Invite a tax accountant to come to your class. Develop a set of questions to ask before the accountant arrives.

2. After you understand more about taxes, discuss these questions:
   - Why do you think Grandfather had not paid his taxes?
   - Why would the tax man want the farm?
   - What would he do with the farm after he got it?

3. Perhaps you can help Grandfather and little Willy figure out how to pay those back taxes. Solve the problems below.

   (A) If Grandfather owes $500.00 in taxes and little Willy has $50.00 in his bank account, how much money does little Willy need to win after he pays $50.00 to enter the race?

   (B) If Grandfather owes $500.00 in taxes for a period of ten years and taxes have remained the same for ten years, how much are Grandfather's taxes each year?

   (C) If Grandfather gives little Willy $20.00 each year for college and Willy already has $50.00 in the bank, how many years will it take little Willy to save for college if his tuition is $310.00?

   (D) If Grandfather's income was $1,000.00 last year and taxes were the yearly amount you figured in problem (B), what is the percentage of tax that Grandfather must pay?

Quiz Time

1. On the back of this paper, write a one-paragraph summary of the major events that happened in chapters 7 and 8. Then complete the questions on the rest of this page.

2. Why does little Willy go to town the evening before the race?

_____

_____

3. What important understanding takes place between Stone Fox and little Willy?

_____

_____

4. Why do little Willy and Searchlight have an uncomfortable night before the race?

_____

_____

5. What are the thoughts running through little Willy's mind on the morning of the race as he rides into town?

_____

_____

6. What surprises Willy when he gets to town?

_____

_____

7. Little Willy notices that Stone Fox's eyes seem to lack the sparkle that little Willy had seen the night before. Explain any reasons you might think of for this change.

_____

_____

_____

8. Explain why the people of the town seem so tense.

_____

_____

_____

9. How does the race begin? At what time?

_____

_____

10. On the back of this paper, write a paragraph or two as if you are giving a news broadcast live, on the scene, at the beginning of the race. Describe the setting and sounds.

Puppets and Pantomime

Puppets

There are many ways to make puppets show action from a story.

Sack puppets are usually made from standard lunch sacks, with a face and hair pasted on the bottom flap of a flattened sack. Your hand is inserted from the upside-down sack bottom, and holes are often cut in the sides of the sack for thumb and little finger extensions. Puppet head movement is made by moving the sack's flap in a flapping motion.

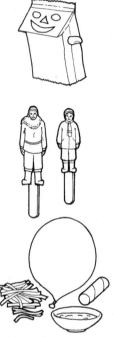

Stick puppets are easy to make with an eight-inch (20 cm) tall picture of your characters. Sketch the character you have chosen, cut it out, and paste it onto a piece of tagboard. Cut around the tagboard again and tape the character onto a ruler or similar piece of wood.

Papier-maché puppets are made with strips of newspaper and wallpaper paste molded over a small balloon for the face and head. The neck is often molded over a short piece of tissue roll that is suspended on a soda bottle and then molded onto the balloon. Clothing is added after the molded head and neck are dry and painted.

Once you have created puppets of Grandfather, little Willy, Stone Fox, Searchlight, and any other characters, you are ready to stage a show.

Remember that puppets must show what they have to communicate without any words from their mouths. They must nod or wag their heads, wave their arms, or otherwise show their feelings by actions. Before you present a puppet show of any scenes from *Stone Fox,* practice some pantomime, or body actions, of your own.

Pantomime

Act out these scenarios and ask your friends to identify what you are doing:

- washing your hands
- walking a tightrope or beam
- testing some very hot water

- smelling a flower
- calling someone on the telephone
- painting a picture

Now, remember how actions need to be done in large movements to convey communication on the stage. Move your puppet in large pantomime movements as you develop a scene.

Extension:

Your puppet(s) may be the right size to add to the Story Mobile you made after reading Chapters 3 and 4. (See page 19 for mobile directions.)

Wyoming Animal Report

In *Stone Fox*, dogs play an important part in the story. There are many animals found in the wilds of Wyoming. A partial list includes deer, caribou, moose, wolves, and elk. With your partner, consult an encyclopedia, a book about a specific animal, magazine articles, or other resource books and research a Wyoming animal of your choice. Use this form below to help you organize your material.

Animal Report

Type of animal _____

Size _____

Height _____

Length _____

Weight _____

Describe its habitat and range. _____

_____

_____

Describe its enemies. _____

_____

_____

Describe any characteristics of its defense. _____

_____

_____

Describe its most interesting feature. _____

_____

_____

List your resources. _____

_____

Draw a picture of the animal in its natural environment. Attach it to your report.

Genre

We use the word genre when we refer to a type, or a kind of writing. Here are some things to look for in different genres:

- **Fairy Tale:** a folk story about real life problems, but involving imaginary characters and magical events

- **Fantasy:** a highly fanciful story about characters, places, and events that, while sometimes believable, do not exist

- **Legend:** a traditional, historical tale of a people, handed down first by word of mouth, later in written form

- **Tall Tale:** a story about impossible or exaggerated happenings related in a matter-of-fact and often humorous way

Activities

Based on the definitions above, in what genre do you believe *Stone Fox* would fit?

_____

Why did you choose that? _____

Fill in each of the boxes of this story plot chart. (The first story is completed as an example.) When you have finished, you will have identified the main points of *Stone Fox*. These points create the problems and solutions in the story.

Who	Wanted	But	So
Three Billy Goats Gruff	to cross the bridge	the troll wanted to eat them	they tricked the troll
Grandfather			
Little Willy			
Stone Fox			

Spuds à la Carte

Potatoes come in many forms and in many products.
Take a note pad and pencil with you and visit the aisles in
a grocery store. Record all the potato products you can
find (chips, soup, French fries, etc.) Staple your list to the
left edge of this page. How many potato products did you
find?

Interesting Information

The potato is solid, yet it is 80% water. The potato is not a root but a tuber that stores food
for the green leaves above ground. Its plant relatives are the tomato, pepper, eggplant,
petunia, and tobacco plants.

Potatoes are low in fat and high in vitamins and minerals. They store extra glucose as starch,
which gives us carbohydrates, essential nutrients for our bodies.

Russia produces the most potatoes, and China is the world's second largest potato grower.
The average American eats 131.4 pounds (59.13 kg) of potatoes a year.

Name the different kinds of potatoes that you like to eat. Using the average amount of 131.4
pounds (59.13 kg), estimate how many pounds of each kind of potato you might eat per year.
(**For example:** If you eat mashed potatoes and French fried potatoes, and you eat mashed
just as often as French fried, you could estimate that you would eat 65.7 pounds, or 29.57 kg
of each kind.)

List: Kinds of potatoes I eat	Estimated lbs. (kg) per year

Quiz Time

1. On the back of this paper, write a one-paragraph summary of the major events that happened in chapters 9 and 10. Then complete the questions on the rest of this page.

2. Describe how Willy and Stone Fox each start off in the big race.

   _____

   _____

3. What shortcut can Willy take in the race course that no one else dares to take?

   _____

   _____

4. How many miles long is the race?

   _____

   _____

   From what point to what point is this in *your* daily travels?

   _____

   _____

5. What does Willy notice when he races past his house?

   _____

   _____

6. Searchlight notices something as they approach town that makes her give a last great effort. What do you think that is?

   _____

   _____

7. What happens to Searchlight as they approach the finish line?

   _____

   _____

8. How does Stone Fox stop the race?

   _____

   _____

9. What do little Willy and Stone Fox have in common that helps Stone Fox be sympathetic toward Willy and Grandfather?

   _____

   _____

10. On the back of this paper, write your own extension of this story, telling what you think will happen in the following year and before the next year's taxes are due.

Landmarks and Topography

The setting for *Stone Fox* has beautiful mountains, a lake, woods, houses, and town buildings. Think of the course that little Willy and the other racers ran and the landmarks that were along the way.

In cooperative learning groups, create a mural of the story setting on a large sheet of butcher paper. Illustrate the mountains, lake, woods, houses, and town buildings that were mentioned in the story.

Use your knowledge of the race mileage and the miles per inch for your mural to recreate the race course. Be sure to include a key to your map to show miles (km) per inch. Use the space below to plan your mural.

Working together, place the landmarks and the race course on the mural. Again, be sure to include a key to your map.

Thinking Clouds

Stone Fox and little Willy have many thoughts as they learn about each other, about themselves and their values, and about life. Imagine that you are Stone Fox or little Willy. What would you be thinking while the events were taking place? Discuss your ideas with a literature group. Then write your predicted thoughts for Stone Fox and for little Willy inside the clouds. Be sure to follow the ideas as listed:

What they learn about **each other**. . .

What they learn about **life**. . .

What they learn about **themselves**. . .

Go, Searchlight, Go!

Searchlight is a very intelligent dog. Look through the story and list behaviors that show you she is smart. Write them here.

_____

_____

_____

_____

_____

_____

_____

Can Searchlight solve problems? Search the story for behaviors that show she can. Write your ideas on the lines below.

The Problem	Searchlight's Solution
_____	_____
_____	_____
_____	_____
_____	_____
_____	_____
_____	_____
_____	_____

Extension:

Read and share a story with your class about a devoted, smart, or unusual dog.
Imagine that the dog you choose to read about dies. Write an obituary for the dog.

Your Life. . . Your List

You can learn something about a character or a person's life if you read the lists they make for themselves.

Imagine that you are Grandfather, little Willy, or Stone Fox. Using the story, make lists for each character and one for yourself.

Grandfather	Little Willy	Stone Fox	You
shopping in town	shopping in town	shopping in town	shopping in town
things to do	things to do	things to do	things to do
"wish list"	"wish list"	"wish list"	"wish list"

What did you learn about each character? What did you learn about yourself? Write your ideas on the back of this paper.

Any Questions?

When you finished reading *Stone Fox,* did you have some questions that were left unanswered? Write them here.

_____

_____

_____

_____

_____

_____

Work in groups or by yourself to prepare possible answers for the questions you asked above or those printed below. When you finish, share your ideas with the class.

- Do any of the other dogsled racers cross the line that Stone Fox draws in the snow?

- What do the people who are watching the race do when Willy picks up Searchlight?

- What does little Willy do after all of the commotion settles down?

- How does little Willy tell Grandfather about the race?

- What is Grandfather's reaction after he is told the news about the race and about Searchlight?

- Does Stone Fox help little Willy bury Searchlight?

- How does Clifford Snyder act when he hears the news?

- How do the children at school act when Willy comes to school?

- Does Grandfather's state of mind and health improve?

- Does Grandfather get to keep the potato farm?

- Do you think Stone Fox will come to Jackson again?

- What will have to happen in future years so little Willy and Grandfather can stay on the farm?

- Do you think Willy will get another dog?

- Will little Willy go to college one day?

Book Report Ideas

There are numerous ways to report on a book once you have read it. After you have finished reading *Stone Fox*, choose one method of reporting on the book that interests you. It may be a way your teacher suggests, an idea of your own, or one of the ways mentioned below.

Character Biography

Choose a character from *Stone Fox*. Using the text and your own imagination, write a short biography for the character. Tell where the character was born, what happened in his or her life, who influenced that life, and what will happen to the character in the future.

Adjective Scramble

Skim the entire story of *Stone Fox*. Choose adjectives that describe the characters, the setting, or the events. Add more adjectives of your own that describe your thoughts and feelings as you read the story. Now sort the adjectives in a way that makes sense to you. (**Example:** adjectives that describe positive, negative, or neutral feelings)

News Report

Write a news article for the local paper in Jackson, Wyoming, telling of the National Dogsled Race, the entrants, the events, and the winner. Remember to focus on who, what, where, when, and why. This should be written in expository style, focusing on the facts.

Write a Poem

Feelings are often expressed in poetry form. Write a ballad about a character in *Stone Fox* or a poem about the dogsled race. A ballad is a poem in verse, often put to music. A rap is a poem with a strong beat, often told with a fast rhythm. You might want to try creating a rap about the dogsled race.

Advice Column

Choose a character from *Stone Fox*. Write an advice column to that character. Think about what questions or problems might be bothering that character and how you could best help the character solve the problem.

TV Review

Think about the story of *Stone Fox* as a movie. Sometimes a movie based on a book changes the scenery, characters, or some of the events. Would you keep this story the same, or would you change parts of it? Write a critical review, explaining what you would keep or change and why.

Daily Log

If Grandfather, little Willy, or Stone Fox kept diaries of their daily events and feelings, what would they write? Choose one character and write a daily entry for two weeks before and after the dogsled race.

Stars

You are a STAR because you have studied this book in depth. Your ideas are unique. Give yourself a star and credit for what you have learned!

Complete the following statements with your own reactions to *Stone Fox*.

Before I read *Stone Fox,* I _____

_____

Some of the things I learned are_____

_____

_____

_____

Because I have read and studied *Stone Fox,* I might want to learn more about _____

_____

_____

My favorite characters were_____

_____

_____

My favorite scene(s) were _____

_____

_____

My reactions to what happened at the end of the story were_____

_____

_____

I would recommend this book to others because _____

_____

_____

"Share the Story" Book Talk

Now that you have finished *Stone Fox*, tell three people you know all about the story in a "book talk" style.

Who will you tell?

_____

_____

_____

Here is the format to help you give a book talk. Do not tell the whole story all over again. A book talk gives just enough information so other people will want to read the story and discover what else happened.

Who? Who are the main characters in *Stone Fox*?

Where? Where does the story take place?

When? During what time of the year do the story events occur? What part of the century is this?

What? What were some of the events in the story?

Often a good story has one big problem that must be solved. This big problem is often the central plot of the story. On the lines below, tell the central plot of the story in just one sentence. Use this idea for your book talk.

_____

_____

_____

_____

You could end your book talk with the following sentence:

"The biggest problem in this story is that _____, and I hope you'll read the story to find out how the problem is solved."

More Ideas

- Design a three dimensional (3-D) model of a dogsled race course. Use homemade clay, papier-mâché, and glossy paper to show hills, trees, lakes, and obstacles.

- Create a map for a dogsled race, with details of miles to be covered, checkpoints for stopping places or timing checks, obstacles, viewing stands, and the finish line. Create a key to the map, showing the distance scale and the icons you have used.

- Write a newspaper advertisement, encouraging people to enter the dogsled race. Show a brief sketch of the race itinerary, the application form to enter the race, and a listing of prizes to be earned.

- Design ribbons, medals, or certificates to give to the participants in a dogsled race. Besides the grand prize, there may be other awards for beauty, grace, generosity, helpfulness, stamina, enthusiasm, etc. Be creative with the variety of awards that might be possible with a dogsled race.

- Using the pictures from the book *Stone Fox* for a model, create a sled that would be suitable for dogsled racing. Use folded, creased, curled, or pasted paper to create your dogsled.

Quiet on the Set

Create a skit from one important scene in *Stone Fox*. For example, a scene might be when the tax collector arrives at the farm. A scene has a definite beginning, middle, and an end, like a little story taken out of a big story. In your skit show how your characters would develop actions and what the characters might say to each other. Use the organizer below to help you.

Create-a-scene Organizer

Event	Setting
Characters	**Costumes**
Scenery	**Props**

Checklist for extras, as needed:

- Video Camera

- Tape Recorder

- Sound Effects

- Lighting

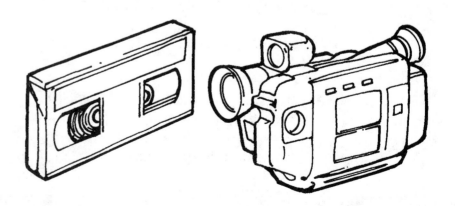

Unit Test

Matching: Write the letter next to the name it matches.

_____ 1. Jackson	A. the mayor's last name
_____ 2. Williams	B. an apprentice potato farmer
_____ 3. Clifford Snyder	C. a woman doctor's last name
_____ 4. Smith	D. a potato farmer
_____ 5. Grandfather	E. a town near the Tetons
_____ 6. Smiley	F. a woman teacher's last name
_____ 7. Stone Fox	G. a Shoshone tribe member
_____ 8. Willy	H. the tax collector

True or False: Write true or false next to each statement below. On the back of this test paper, explain why each false answer is false.

_____ 1. Grandfather has no way to communicate when he is in bed.

_____ 2. Doc Smith wants someone else to take care of Grandfather.

_____ 3. Searchlight seems to understand people.

_____ 4. Willy uses his college money to harvest the potatoes.

_____ 5. Willy goes to school on the school bus.

_____ 6. Grandfather knows about the past taxes being overdue.

_____ 7. Only nine sleds enter the dogsled race.

_____ 8. Everyone in town wants Willy to enter the race.

_____ 9. Willy gets a black eye by bumping his head on something.

_____ 10. Searchlight is always ahead of the Samoyeds as she runs.

Short Answers:

1. What kind of a relationship do Grandfather and Willy have? _____

_____

2. What causes Grandfather to go to bed and not talk? _____

_____

Response

Explain what is happening and the meaning of each of these quotations from *Stone Fox*.

Chapter 1:   "It happens when a person gives up. Gives up on life. For whatever reason. Starts up here in the mind first; then it spreads to the body. It's a real sickness, all right. And there's no cure except in the person's own mind."

Chapter 2:   "And Searchlight seemed to know what was going on, for she would lick Grandfather's hand every time he made a sign."

Chapter 3:   "If your teacher don't know—you ask me. If I don't know—you ask the library. If the library don't know then you've really got yourself a good question!"

Chapter 4:   "Grandfather's eyes were wide open and fixed on the ceiling. He looked much older and much more tired than he had this morning."

Chapter 5:   "Little Willy had the will. Now all he had to do was find the way."

Chapter 6:   " 'You must be funning, boy.' The mayor laughed twice and blotted his neck."

Chapter 7:   "Little Willy backed over to the barn door, still holding his eye. 'I'm sorry we both can't win,' he said."

Chapter 8:   " 'Yes, sir,' he remembered Grandfather saying. 'There are some things in this world worth dying for.' "

Chapter 9:   "Grandfather was better. Tears of joy rolled down little Willy's smiling face. Everything was going to be all right. And then Stone Fox made his move."

Chapter 10: "With the heel of his moccasin Stone Fox drew a long line in the snow. Then he walked back over to his sled and pulled out his rifle."

Conversations

Work together to write and perform the conversation and actions that might have occurred in each of the following situations.

- Grandfather dressed as a scarecrow in the garden and Willy took a long time to catch on. (2 people)

- Little Willy and Searchlight discovered that Grandfather wouldn't get up in the morning. (3 people)

- Doc Smith visits and gives advice to little Willy and Searchlight. (3 people)

- Grandfather and little Willy develop their signals for Grandfather to communicate. (2 people)

- Searchlight shows little Willy that she will help with the potato harvest. (2 people)

- Clifford Snyder visits the farm and tells Grandfather, little Willy, and Searchlight what will happen to the farm if they don't pay the taxes. (4 people)

- Little Willy visits with Doc Smith and shares the news about the past due taxes. (2 people)

- Little Willy visits with Mr. Foster at the bank about getting money for taxes. (2 people)

- Little Willy visits Lester at the General Store, discovering the poster. (2 people)

- Little Willy and Searchlight stop to visit the Samoyeds in the barn, and Stone Fox comes in. (3 people)

Work in pairs to write spontaneous conversations by passing a shared piece of paper between you and your partner. One of you take the role of either Willy or Stone Fox. The other person initiates the conversation with comments such as the following:

"Willy, I can't understand how you could manage to harvest all those potatoes alone." (Pass the paper, and your partner—playing the role of Willy—answers you, then passes the paper back to you for your additional comments or questions.)

"Stone Fox, I wonder why. . . "

"Willy, I thought something would happen when you. . . "

"Willy, I know the feeling of _____ because. . . "

"Stone Fox, I think you should be proud because. . . "

"Willy, I'm sorry about. . . "

Annotated Bibliography

Dogsled Racing

Flanders, Noel K. *The Joy of Running Sled Dogs: A Step-by-Step Guide.* (Alpine Publications, 1989), 108 pages. This book gives advice on selecting, training, and caring for sled dogs and equipment.

Crisman, Ruth. *Racing the Iditarod Trail.* (Macmillan, 1993), 72 pages. This book highlights the history and origins of the Iditarod.

O'Dell, Scott. *Black Star, Bright Dawn.* (Houghton Mifflin, 1988), 134 pages. Bright Dawn must face the challenge of the Iditarod dogsled race alone when her father is injured.

Paulsen, Gary. *Dogteam.* (Delacorte, 1993), 32 pages. This picture book portrays the excitement, the danger, and the beauty of a night run.

Paulsen, Gary. *Woodsong.* (Bradbury Press, 1990), 132 pages. For a rugged outdoor man and his family, life in northern Minnesota is an adventure involving wolves, deer, and sled dogs. Paulsen includes an account of the author's first Iditarod, a dogsled race across Alaska.

Seibert, Patricia. *Mush!: Across Alaska in the World's Longest Sled-Dog Race.* (Milbrook Press, 1992), 32 pages. Seibert describes the annual Iditarod dogsled race in Alaska and the sled dogs that compete in it.

Stories About Dogs

Davidson, Margaret. *Five True Dog Stories.* (Scholastic, 1977), 46 pages. These are true stories about five real dogs.

Lewis, J. Patrick. *One Dog Day.* (Macmillan, 1993), 64 pages. A pet collie is entered in a coon dog contest.

Standiford, Natalie. *The Bravest Dog Ever: The True Story of Balto.* (Random House [*Step into Reading*], 1989), 48 pages. Balto, a sled dog, saved Nome, Alaska, in 1925 from a diphtheria epidemic by delivering medicine through a raging snowstorm.

Wels, Bryon G. *Animal Heroes: Stories of Courageous Family Pets and Animals of the Wild.* (Macmillan, 1979), 145 pages.

Stories About Courage and Determination

Arnosky, Jim. *Gray Boy.* (Lothrop, 1991), 82 pages. A young boy must cope with a tragic, terrible truth about his beloved pet dog, Gray Boy, a last gift to him from his late father.

Cleary, Beverly. *Strider.* (Morrow, 1991), 179 pages. In a series of diary entries, Leigh tells how he comes to terms with his parent's divorce, acquires joint custody of an abandoned dog, and joins the track team at school.

Naylor, Phyllis Reynolds. *Shiloh.* (Atheneum, 1991), 144 pages. When he finds a lost beagle in the hills behind his West Virginia home, Marty tries to hide it from his family and the dog's real owner, a mean-spirited man known to shoot deer out of season and to mistreat his dogs.

Whelan, Gloria. *Silver.* (Random House [*Stepping Stone*], 1988), 58 pages. Even though her puppy is the runt of the litter from her father's prize sled-racing dog, ten-year-old Rachel plans to train him to become a champion racer and determines to track him down when he mysteriously disappears.

Stone Fox

Answer Key

Page 12

1. Accept appropriate responses.
2. Grandfather dresses up as the scarecrow out in the garden.
3. Willy is late getting up in the morning, and Grandfather had warned him that if he was late for breakfast, he would have to eat with the chickens.
4. He tells her that Grandfather has gone to bed without playing the harmonica.
5. He is very sad when he hears Willy talk about the enjoyable things they did together.
6. She says that Grandfather does not want to live anymore.
7. Grandfather gives hand and finger signals for yes, no, hunger, and water.
8. Searchlight wears a harness and pulls the plow to dig up the plants. Then Willy picks up the potatoes.
9. Searchlight is a very smart dog who can understand how to help Willy and Grandfather.
10. Accept appropriate responses about Grandfather's sickness and who should take care of him.

Page 17

1. Accept any appropriate responses.
2. "If your teacher don't know—you ask me. If I don't know—you ask the library. If the library don't know—then you've really got yourself a good question!"
3. He chops wood and buys enough food for winter.
4. He has saved money for Willy's college education.
5. When the church clock strikes 6:00, Searchlight and Willy run from town to home as fast as they can.
6. The tax collector, Clifford Snyder, is

waiting.
7. Grandfather doesn't move his hand or even his fingers.
8. The description should include something about Clifford Snyder being mean, a bully, demanding, or arrogant.
9. If Grandfather doesn't pay the $500 in back taxes, the state will take the farm.
10. Accept any appropriate response regarding Willy's predicament.

Page 20

1. Sled 1—34.3, Sled 2—38.3, Sled 3—35.3, Sled 4—34.3
2. Sled 2
3. 34.3
4. 2
5. 333 minutes (Add the times in day 1; divide by 4 to get the average time for 5 miles. Multiply by 9 to get the average time for 45 miles).

Extension: (1) 37, 37.5, 32.25 (2) 30

Page 22

1. Accept any appropriate response.
2. When you want to do something badly enough, you should try to figure out a way to do it.
3. He thinks the money from selling the farm will pay the taxes and then the state will not take it.
4. Willy sees a poster advertising the National Dogsled Race with prize money of $500.
5. Accept any appropriate response.
6. He uses his college savings from the bank.
7. He sees a very large man with five beautiful white Samoyeds.
8. He is angry because of the way his tribe has been treated.
9. He wants to earn enough money from his racing so he can buy back land for his Shoshone tribe.
10. Accept any appropriate response.

Answer Key

Page 25

1. underground
2. need a mound of dirt around each plant
3. a special piece of another potato
4. in almost all the countries of the world
5. Answers will vary. The teacher may want to give each student a piece of raw potato to try.
6. 30

Page 26

1. Questions will vary.
2. A. He did not have a crop that was large enough or good enough or the price for potatoes was very low.

   B. It is state law that a farm, land, or a house can be sold to pay for the back taxes that are owed.

   C. He would sell it at an auction and pay the taxes
3. A. $550; $50 to put back into savings and $500 to pay taxes
   B. $50.00
   C. 13 years
   D. 5%

Page 27

1. Accept any appropriate response.
2. He goes to get some medicine for Grandfather.
3. Stone Fox learns that Willy needs to win the race money to save his Grandfather's land, and he learns how determined Willy is.
4. Willy's eye is hurting him, and when he is restless, Searchlight is restless, too.
5. Willy thinks about the beautiful country that he lives in and how Grandfather loves it.
6. There are people all over town, ready to watch the race.

7. Accept any appropriate response.
8. Accept any appropriate response.
9. The race begins at 10:00 when the mayor fires his pistol.
10. Accept any appropriate response that is written in a news broadcast style of writing.

Page 32

1. Accept any appropriate response.
2. Willy and Searchlight start with a lurch, far ahead of the others. Stone Fox starts off slowly and is last.
3. Willy and Searchlight run across the frozen lake instead of following a turn around it.
4. It is ten miles. Answers will vary.
5. He sees Grandfather sitting up in bed and looking out of the window.
6. It is a building that looks like Grandfather's farmhouse.
7. She tries to run as fast as she can, and she dies of heart failure.
8. Stone Fox draws a line across the snow with his boot, takes his rifle out of his sled, and fires a shot in the air to stop the other racers.
9. They both have the feeling of losing their land to the government.
10. Accept any appropriate response.

Page 43

Matching	True or False
1. E	1. F
2. F	2. T
3. H	3. T
4. C	4. F
5. D	5. F
6. A	6. T
7. G	7. T
8. B	8. F
	9. F
	10. F

48